T5-BYN-148

kids draw™

KNIGHTS, KINGS, QUEENS & DRAGONS

CHRISTOPHER HART

WATSON-GUPTILL PUBLICATIONS/NEW YORK

For Dom and Santa

Senior Editor: Candace Raney
Editors: Alisa Palazzo and Julie Mazur
Designers: Bob Fillie, Graphiti Design, Inc. and Sivan Earnest
Production Manager: Hector Campbell

Front and back cover illustrations by Christopher Hart
Text copyright © 2001 Christopher Hart
Illustrations copyright © 1999 Christopher Hart

The materials appearing in this book are copyrighted in the name
of the author. They may not be reproduced or used in any format
or for any purpose without the written permission of the author.

First published in 2001 by
Watson-Guptill Publications,
a division of VNU Business Media, Inc.,
770 Broadway, New York, N.Y. 10003
www.wgpub.com

Based on *How to Draw Knights, Kings, Queens & Dragons,*
published in 1999 by Watson-Guptill Publications

Library of Congress Card Number: 00-111778

All rights reserved. No part of this publication may be reproduced or used
in any form or by any means—graphic, electronic, or mechanical, including
photocopying, recording, or information storage-and-retrieval systems—
without the written permission of the publisher.

Printed in Singapore

First printing, 2001

2 3 4 5 6 7 8 / 08 07 06 05

CONTENTS

INTRODUCTION

Greetings, noble cartoonists of the round table! I ask you to take up pencils and join me on a quest, a quest to draw brave knights, beautiful princesses, wise queens, and evil dragons.

To accomplish this task, it takes a person who is pure of heart, steady of hand, who has a keen eye and lots of paper. I sense that you are, indeed, that person. I hereby dub thee, knight of the cartoonist's table!

Inside this book, you'll find a medieval village of olde. King Arthur is there, along with Merlin, dashing princes, brave princesses, and fierce dragons. You'll meet some of the townsfolk who live outside the castle, and you'll learn about medieval weapons, like armor, swords, and shields. Did you know that horses wore armor, too?

As you follow along, you'll also learn important drawing skills. For example, you'll learn how to give your characters different body types. Knights are usually tall and strong, but there are also young knights (squires) and older knights. Kings can be short and fat or tall and skinny. Queens can be tall and elegant or old and stodgy. In fact, you'll be able to draw any kind of character you want. The possibilities are endless.

So turn the page and let's take a trip back in time, learning to draw along the way!

KNIGHTS

In many stories of old, the fate of an entire kingdom rested on the shoulders of a single brave knight.

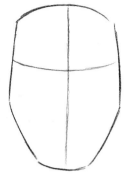

The knight's jaw is wide and powerful. His forehead is on the small side.

The eyes rest on the horizontal guideline. The bridge of the nose falls where the horizontal and vertical lines cross.

Give him heavy eyebrows and strong cheekbones.

His hairstyle and beard should be typical of medieval times.

Rugged Knight

Let's begin with the head of a basic, strong knight. Start with the front view.

Add some clothes, and you're done!

The side view of a knight should have sharp angles. This will make him look strong—as if he were made of stone.

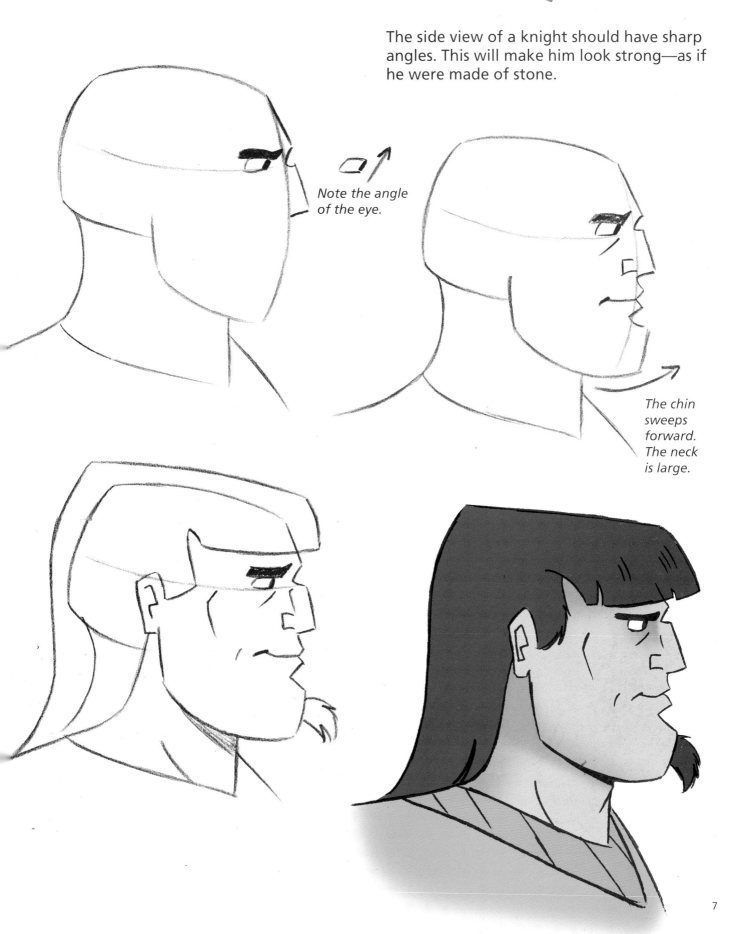

Note the angle of the eye.

The chin sweeps forward. The neck is large.

Other Head Angles

Once you have the basic structure of the head down, you can create poses in any angle. Just think of the head as a solid block that you can rotate in space.

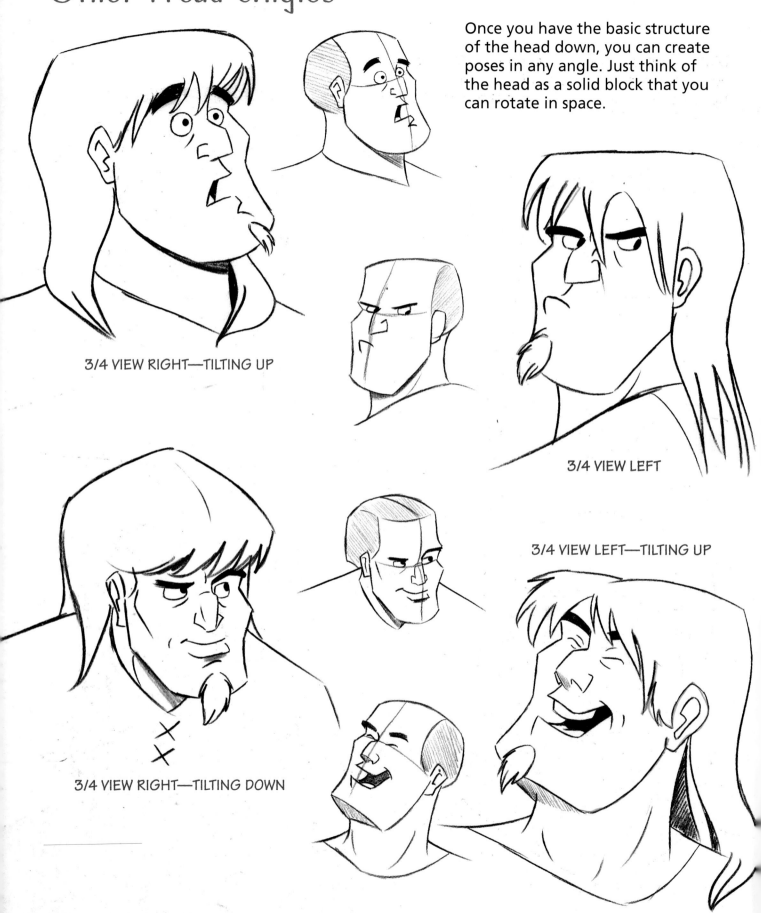

3/4 VIEW RIGHT—TILTING UP

3/4 VIEW LEFT

3/4 VIEW LEFT—TILTING UP

3/4 VIEW RIGHT—TILTING DOWN

Many knights were only teenagers. To make your knight look younger, give him an upturned nose and smaller cheekbones.

Basic Knight Body

To draw the body, break it down into major masses and shapes.

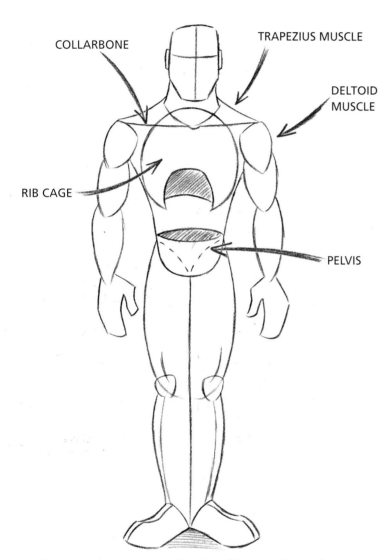

COLLARBONE

TRAPEZIUS MUSCLE

DELTOID MUSCLE

RIB CAGE

PELVIS

The trapezius connects the shoulders to the neck. It is large on strong people and small on weaker ones.

The deltoid has a teardrop shape. It connects the shoulder to the upper arm.

The collarbone looks like a line that runs across the top of the chest.

The rib cage is rounded and hollow. It holds the abdominal muscles.

The pelvis is the "hip" bone.

When drawing a pose from the side, tilt the chest (rib cage) up and the hips (pelvis) down. This will help your character look balanced.

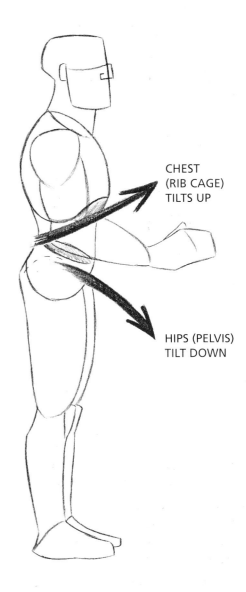

CHEST
(RIB CAGE)
TILTS UP

HIPS (PELVIS)
TILT DOWN

Simplified Body Constructions

Try using what you've learned to draw all sorts of characters. Notice that large figures have large rib cages, while thinner figures have narrow ones.

EVIL COURTIER

TORTURER

GALLANT KNIGHT

FAIR MAIDEN

SAD KNIGHT

Stress Points

To draw an exciting pose, certain parts of the body must bend and show tension. These are called *stress points.* Here are some examples.

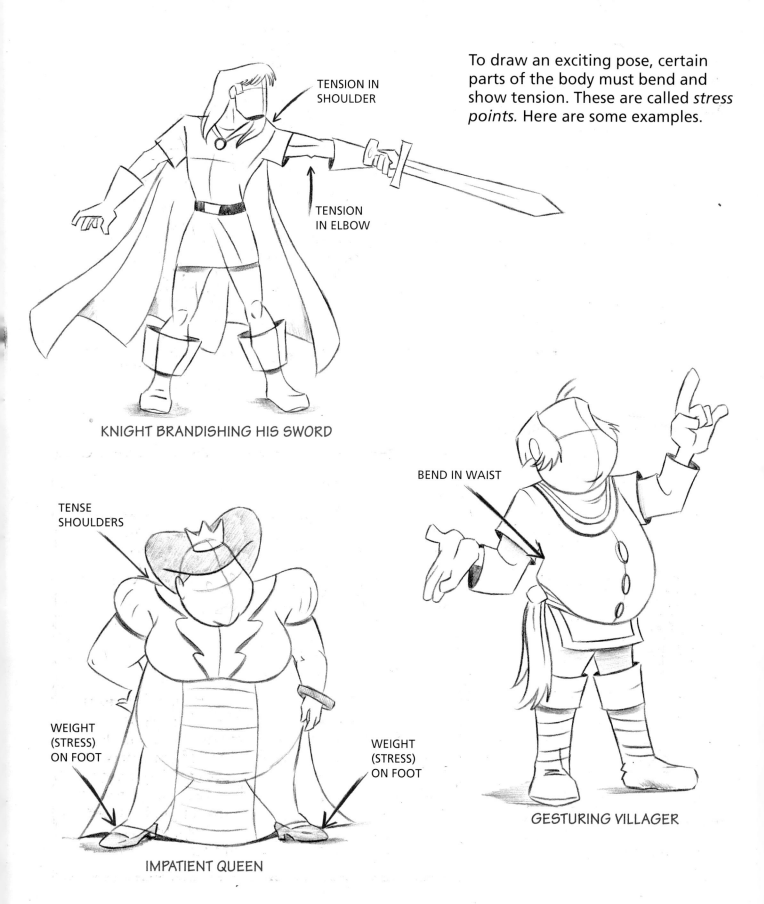

TENSION IN SHOULDER

TENSION IN ELBOW

KNIGHT BRANDISHING HIS SWORD

BEND IN WAIST

GESTURING VILLAGER

TENSE SHOULDERS

WEIGHT (STRESS) ON FOOT

WEIGHT (STRESS) ON FOOT

IMPATIENT QUEEN

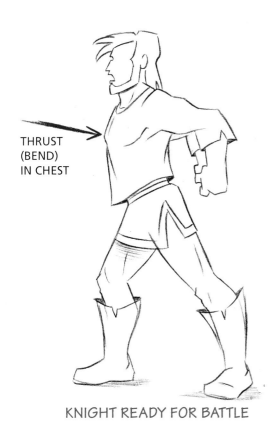

THRUST
(BEND)
IN CHEST

KNIGHT READY FOR BATTLE

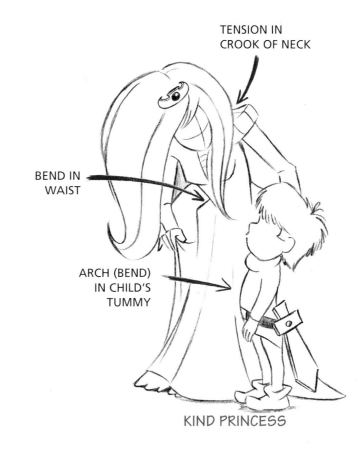

TENSION IN
CROOK OF NECK

BEND IN
WAIST

ARCH (BEND)
IN CHILD'S
TUMMY

KIND PRINCESS

HUNCHED
SHOULDER

HUNCHED
SHOULDER

WALKING HERMIT

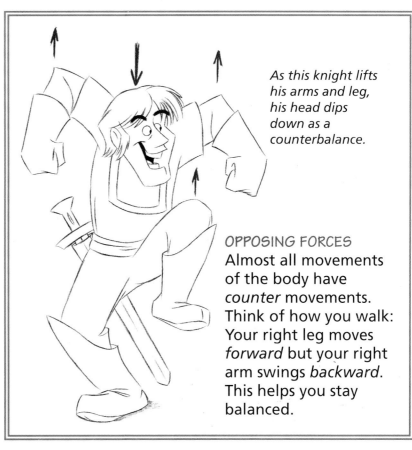

As this knight lifts his arms and leg, his head dips down as a counterbalance.

OPPOSING FORCES
Almost all movements of the body have *counter* movements. Think of how you walk: Your right leg moves *forward* but your right arm swings *backward*. This helps you stay balanced.

Medieval Body Types

The type of body you give your character will help show what type of person he or she is.

SQUIRE
Young and thin.

KNIGHT
Muscular and strong.

KING
Round and fat.

PRINCESS
Young and beautiful.

The Squire

Life in a medieval castle was not all glamorous. The teenage boys who worked there spent most of their time cleaning up horse droppings and tending to livestock. But every once in a while, a boy would get the chance to help a knight. If the boy was good enough, he became a *squire*—an apprentice knight. Squires helped the knights in battle.

Funny Knights

Not all knights have to be strong and handsome. Have fun with your characters!

Knight-and-Squire Comedy Team

Knights and squires make natural comedy duos because their bodies are so different. One is big and the other small—just like lots of real comedy teams.

ARMOR

Knights wore armor for protection when they went into battle. Armor is heavy and bulky. A knight wearing it could only move slowly and with a limited range of motion.

When the visor is down, the eye slots are just visible above it.

The Helmet

The helmet rests on a metal shoulder piece. The visor can be lowered for protection, or raised to see better. Eye slots are built into the visor or are just above it.

When the visor is raised, the eye slots disappear.

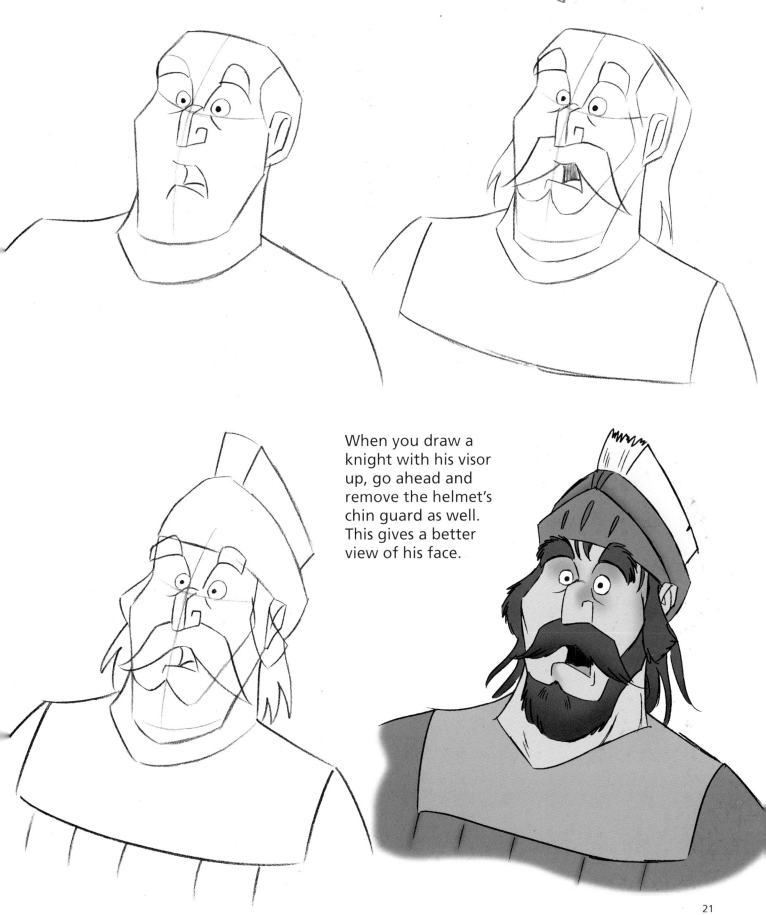

When you draw a knight with his visor up, go ahead and remove the helmet's chin guard as well. This gives a better view of his face.

Types of Helmets

Here are some styles of actual helmets used by knights in battle. You can make your helmets as fancy or plain as you want.

AXE STYLE

TOTAL FACE SHIELD

NOSE GUARD

Chain mail was armor made of metal links or rings, like that shown hanging from this helmet. Chain mail was more flexible than plate armor. It made it easier for knights to move and bend.

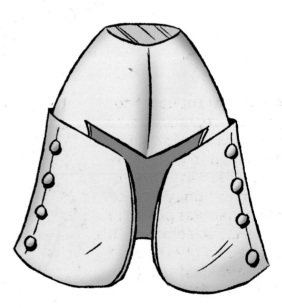

BUCKET STYLE

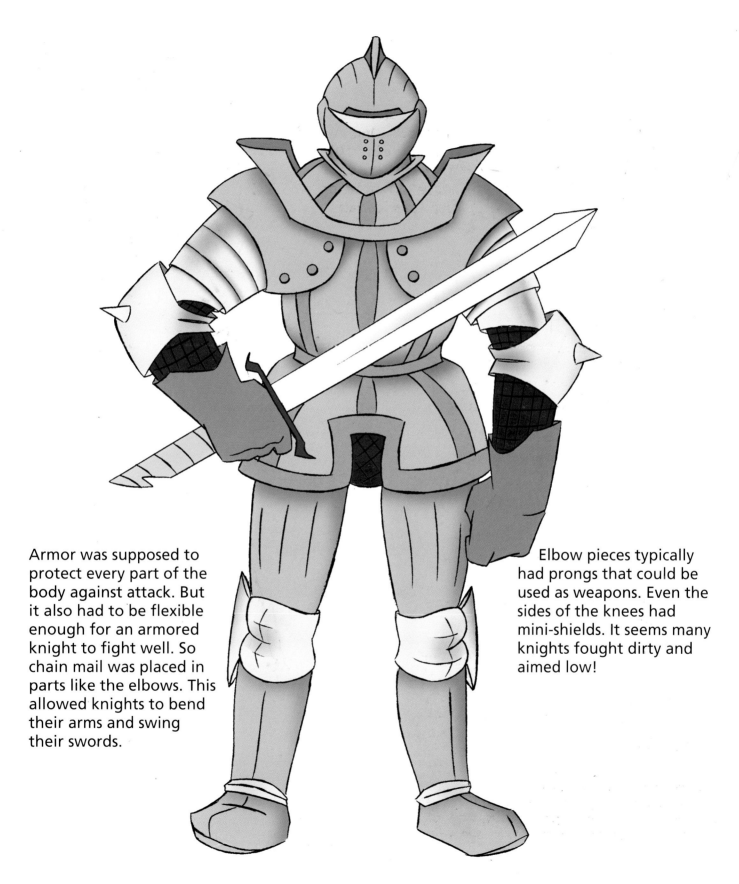

Armor was supposed to protect every part of the body against attack. But it also had to be flexible enough for an armored knight to fight well. So chain mail was placed in parts like the elbows. This allowed knights to bend their arms and swing their swords.

Elbow pieces typically had prongs that could be used as weapons. Even the sides of the knees had mini-shields. It seems many knights fought dirty and aimed low!

Simplified Armor

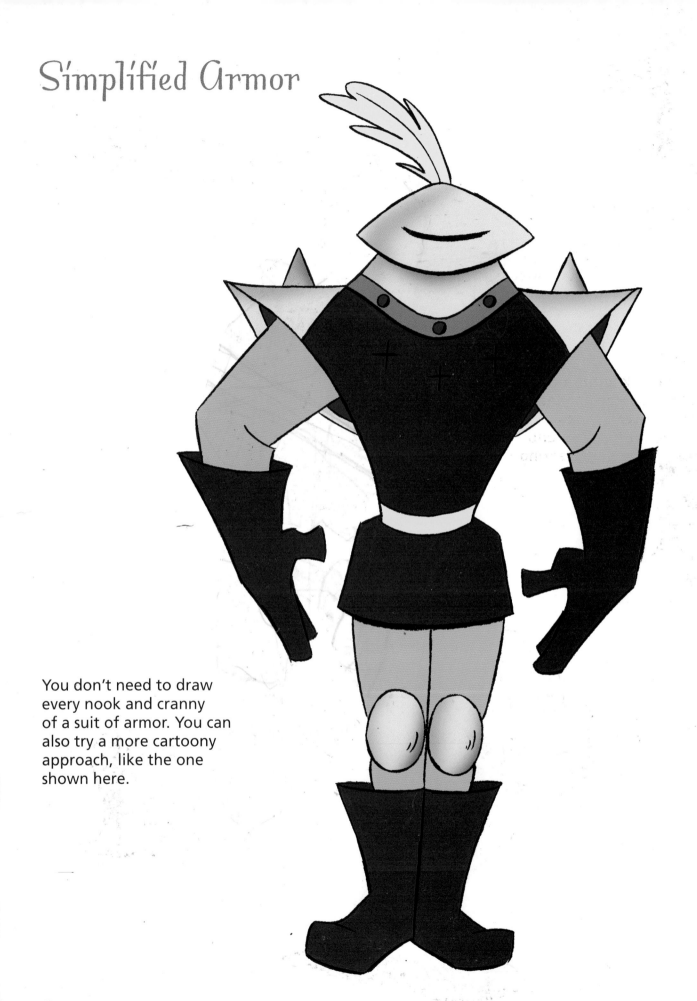

You don't need to draw
every nook and cranny
of a suit of armor. You can
also try a more cartoony
approach, like the one
shown here.

Sometimes, knights just strapped on small plates of armor over their clothes. This was much lighter and more flexible than wearing a whole suit.

Swords and Spears

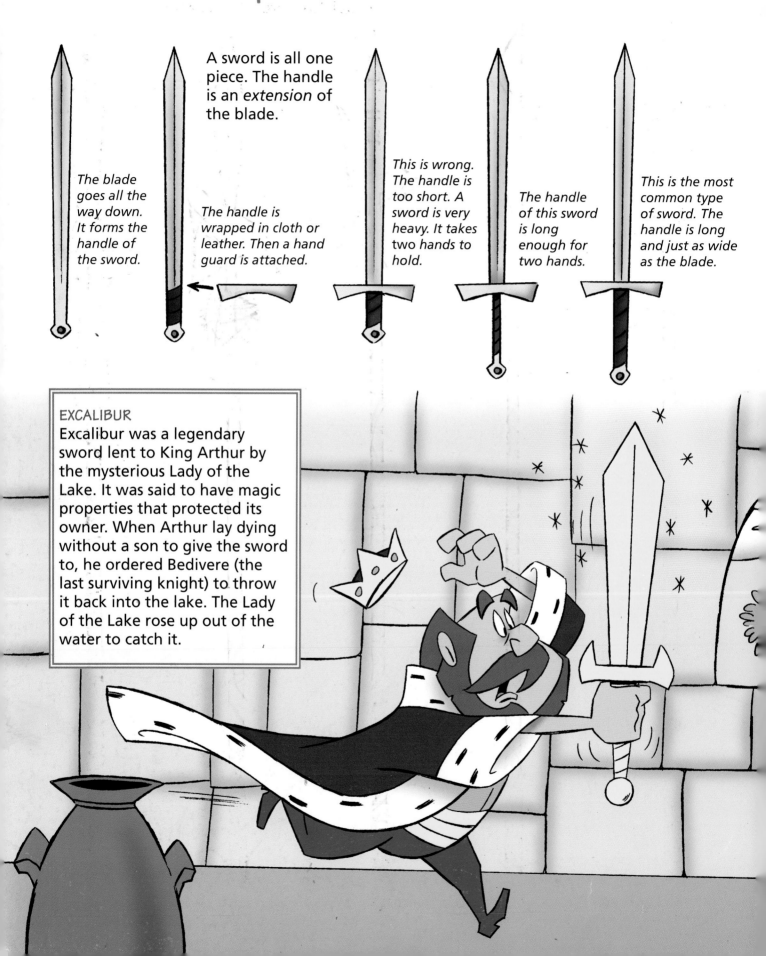

A sword is all one piece. The handle is an *extension* of the blade.

The blade goes all the way down. It forms the handle of the sword.

The handle is wrapped in cloth or leather. Then a hand guard is attached.

This is wrong. The handle is too short. A sword is very heavy. It takes two hands to hold.

The handle of this sword is long enough for two hands.

This is the most common type of sword. The handle is long and just as wide as the blade.

EXCALIBUR
Excalibur was a legendary sword lent to King Arthur by the mysterious Lady of the Lake. It was said to have magic properties that protected its owner. When Arthur lay dying without a son to give the sword to, he ordered Bedivere (the last surviving knight) to throw it back into the lake. The Lady of the Lake rose up out of the water to catch it.

Spears were used in hunting and in battle. The handles were wooden. The blades were metal. Here are a few examples.

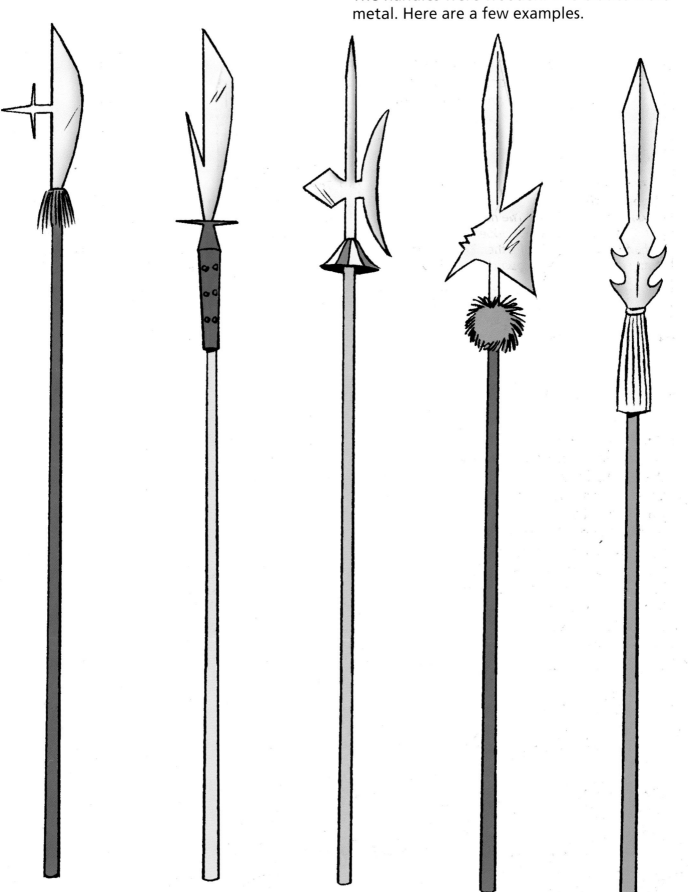

Capes and Jackets

Since fireplaces were the only sources of heat, medieval castles were very cold. Warm clothing was a necessity. Cloaks like these could be worn alone or over a suit of armor.

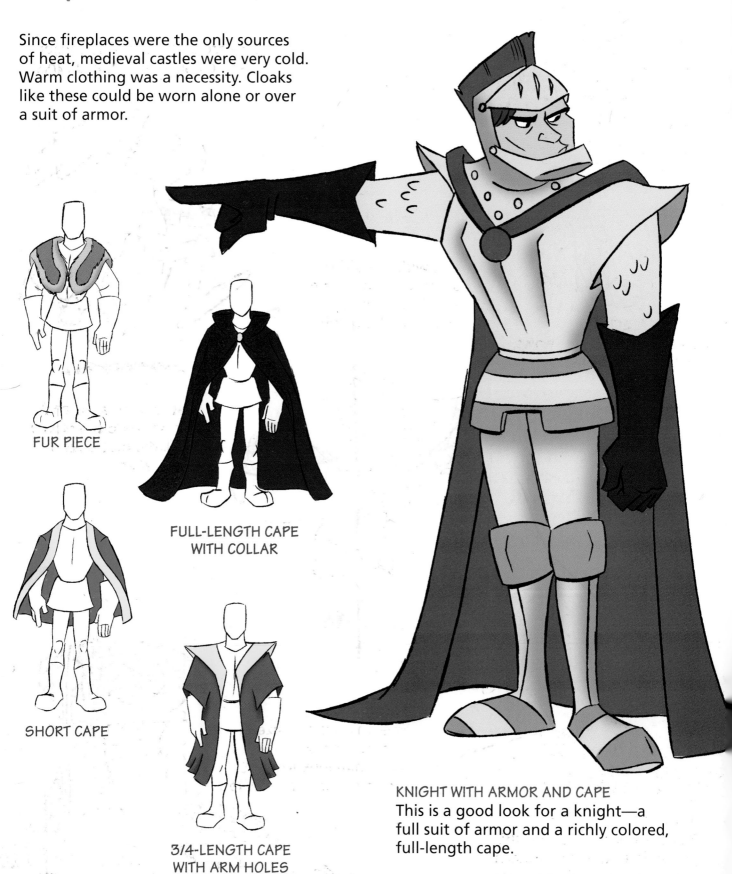

FUR PIECE

FULL-LENGTH CAPE WITH COLLAR

SHORT CAPE

3/4-LENGTH CAPE WITH ARM HOLES

KNIGHT WITH ARMOR AND CAPE
This is a good look for a knight—a full suit of armor and a richly colored, full-length cape.

Funny Armored Knights

Here are a few cartoony versions of some less-than-noble knights.

SMART ALECK
This guy's big nose shows us that he's a jokester.

BRAWNY
Use wide shoulders, short legs, and a very small head for a strong-looking knight.

GOOFY
Draw skinny arms and legs with too-big elbow and knee plates for a funny effect.

WELL-FED
Pity the poor horse that this guy saddles up! His stomach hangs way over his belt line.

POWDER KEG
This knight's oversized sword, cape, and helmet make him look like he's trying on his dad's clothes.

Armored Horses

A knight's horse was like his getaway car, so he protected it with its own suit of armor. Only the horse's upper body was covered—never the legs. Notice the extra bump at the back for the tail.

Facial armor plates protected the horse's head.

Cartoony Armored Knight and Steed

This horse isn't too thrilled about going into battle! His hood of mail makes him look dumb and self-conscious, like a poodle in one of those ridiculous doggy sweaters.

ROYALTY

While a man could earn knighthood (by being an apprentice), he could only be born into royalty. The crown was passed down from father to son. Evil, power-hungry relatives were always plotting to take over the throne for themselves.

King Arthur: The Classic King

King Arthur is one of the most enduring characters of all time. Here you see him as a young man (left) and a bit older (opposite). King Arthur was kind, noble, and courageous. He was also a bit too trusting—he was betrayed by his best friend (Sir Lancelot), his wife (Guinevere), his half sister (Morgan Le Fay), and his son (Mordred)!

Legend tells us that King Arthur was killed in battle by Mordred, who also died in the fight.

Jolly King

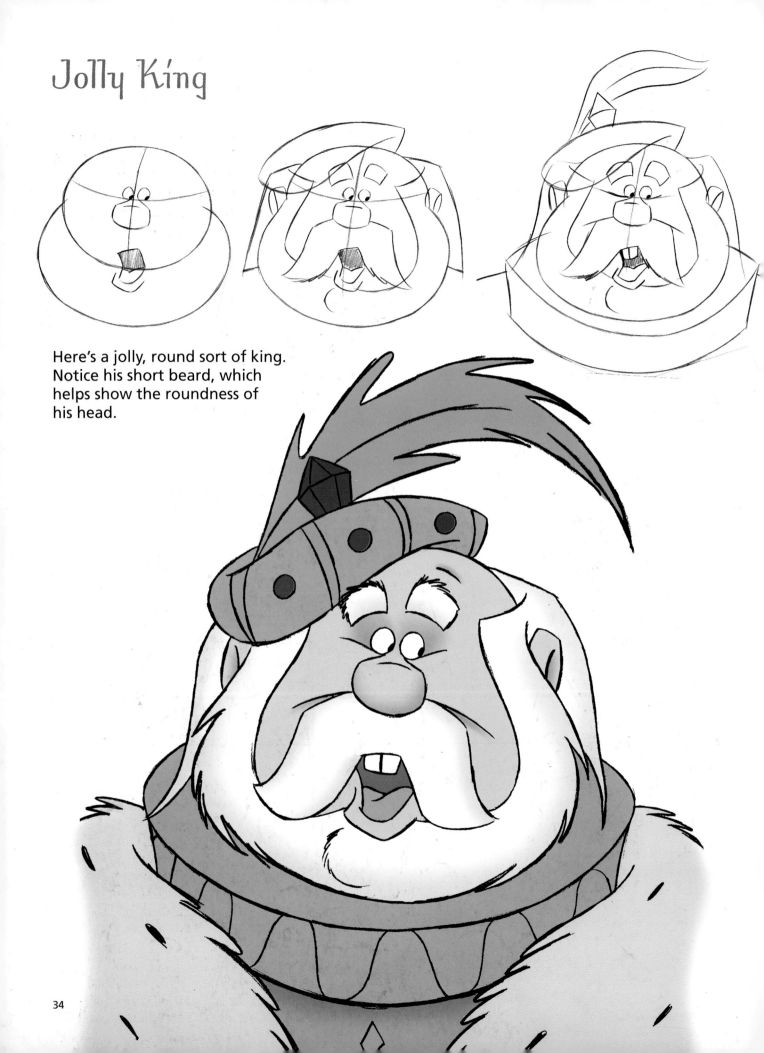

Here's a jolly, round sort of king.
Notice his short beard, which
helps show the roundness of
his head.

Kind (but Stupid) King

How about a king who's kind, but stupid? This guy is easily handled by his wicked advisers. Draw heavy eyelids to make his eyes look sleepy.

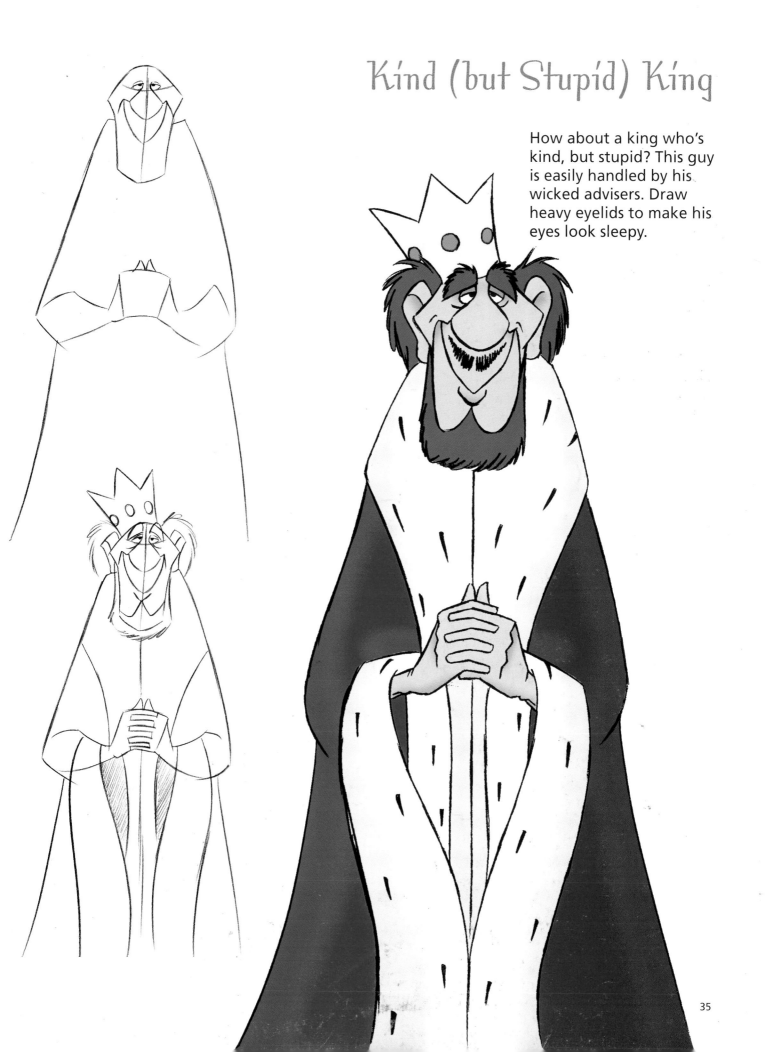

Old Warrior King

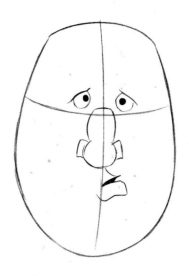

During medieval times, all kings were knights as well. Here is a king with his hood of chain mail.

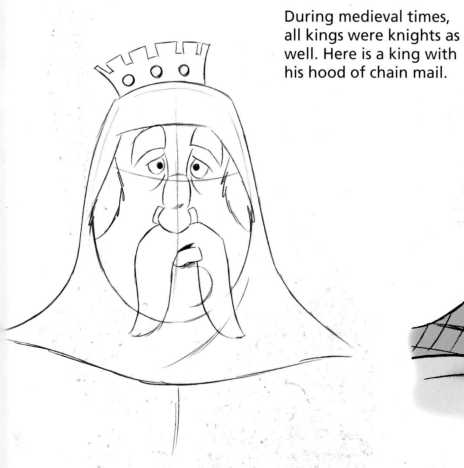

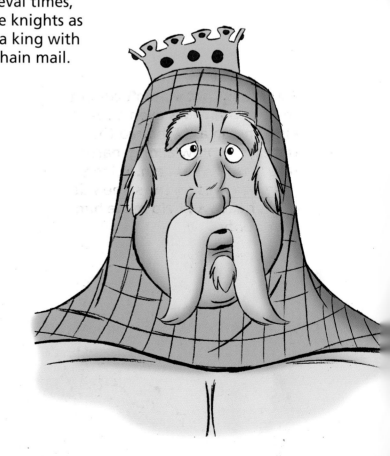

Unready King

Some kings just weren't cut out to rule. There was even a real king known as "Ethelred the Unready"! Draw a long, narrow face with a weak chin. A long nose and eyes on the same side of his head will help make him look goofy.

37

Forgetful King

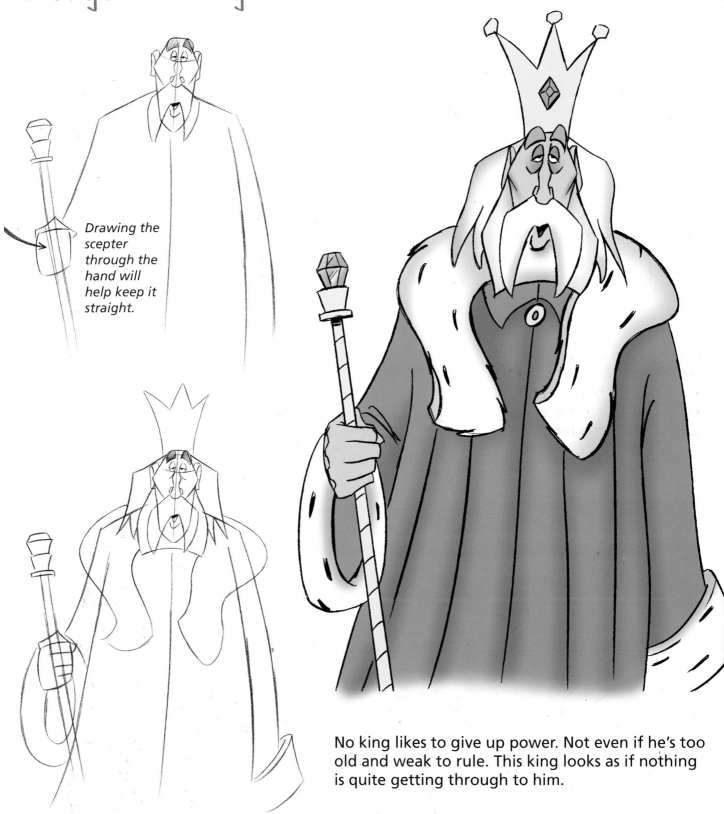

Drawing the scepter through the hand will help keep it straight.

No king likes to give up power. Not even if he's too old and weak to rule. This king looks as if nothing is quite getting through to him.

The evil king is large and impressive. His hair is slightly messy, giving him a wild look. His eyebrows are heavy and he has a low forehead.

Classic Queen

To draw a classic queen, use soft angles. The chin narrows but never comes to a complete point. The neck is thin and graceful. Give her large eyes, with a single dark line for her eyelid and eyelashes. Draw the nose lightly. And make sure her lips are full.

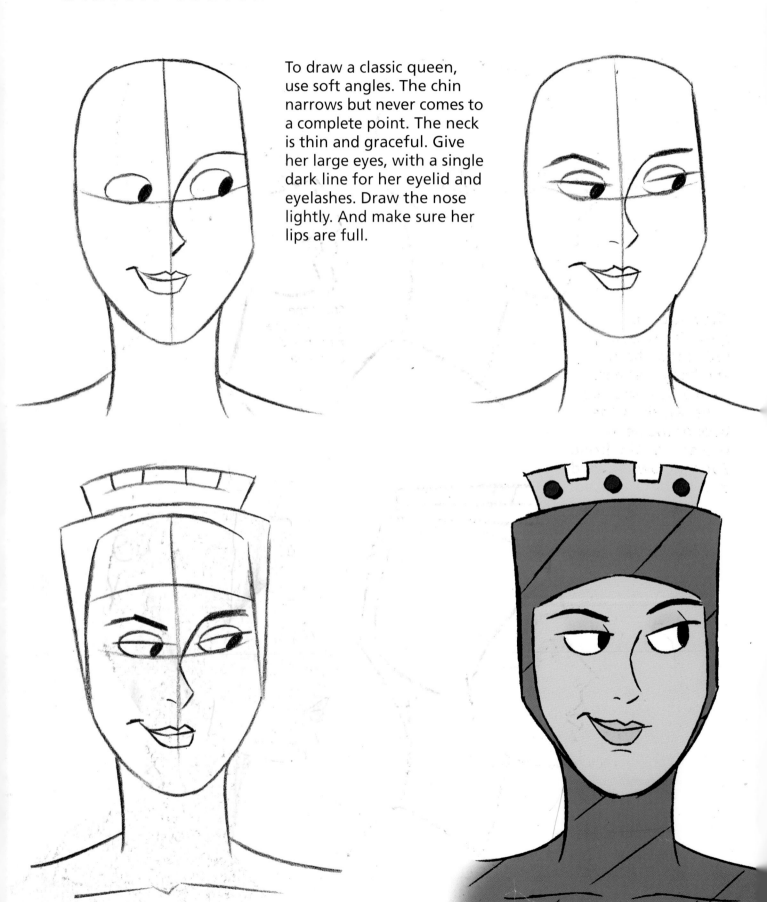

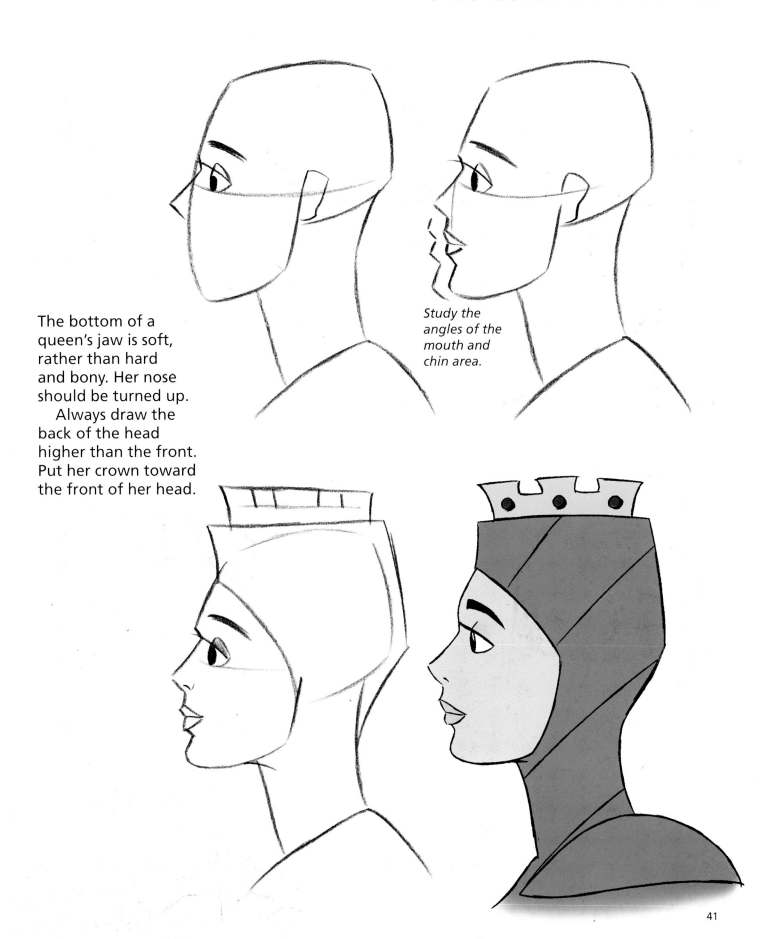

The bottom of a queen's jaw is soft, rather than hard and bony. Her nose should be turned up.

Always draw the back of the head higher than the front. Put her crown toward the front of her head.

Study the angles of the mouth and chin area.

The Queen's Figure

Start by drawing the major masses: the rib cage and the pelvis. Her waist is narrow and her hips are wide. Her shoulders are square but not muscular. In a side view, some of her back is visible behind her shoulders.

It may be tempting to draw your queen's long, flowing dress without first deciding where her hips and legs go. This is a bad idea. Lightly draw the underlying figure first. Then add the dress and erase the legs.

Thrones were carved out of wood. They were not the kind of cozy chairs you'd curl up in with a good book. An evil scheme seems that much more wicked if it is hatched while the queen is on her throne.

The Prince

To draw a prince, just draw a young knight and
dress him up in royal clothes. He doesn't need to
wear a crown. Avoid beards and mustaches—
they will make him look older.

The Princess

Princesses don't have to wear crowns all the time. This princess is wearing a hat-and-veil combination that was also common. Her hairstyle was trendy in the 1400s.

Princess from a Lesser Kingdom

Not all kingdoms were filthy rich. A princess from a smaller kingdom would be more likely to go for barefoot walks in the forest. She'd have long, flowing hair and wear loose-fitting dresses.

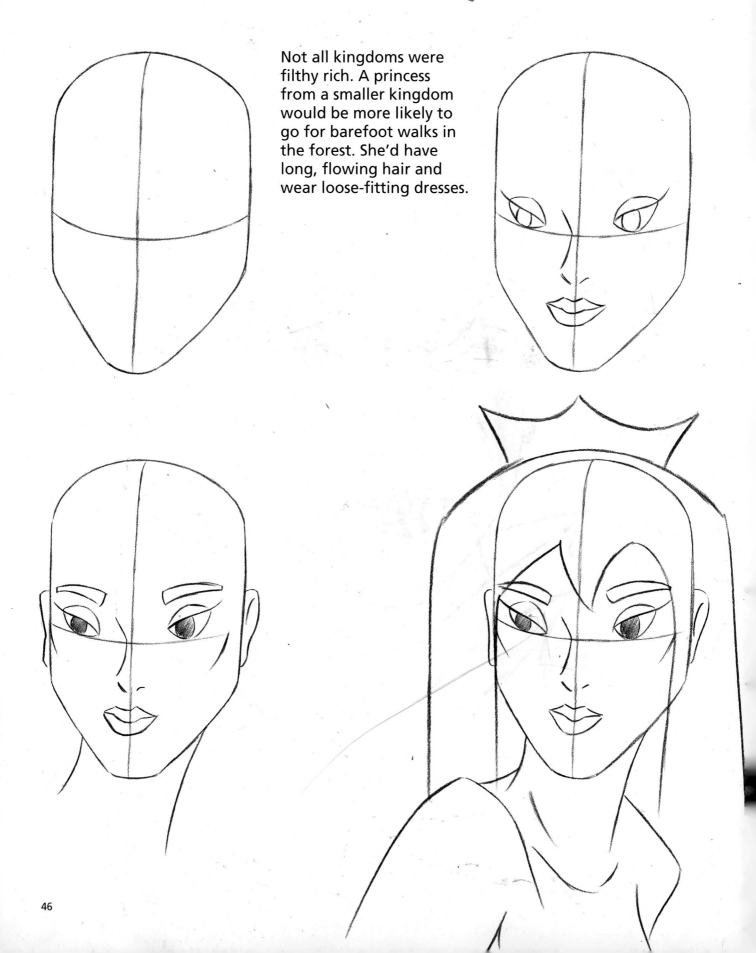

The Princess as a Little Girl

SOMEDAY...
Every little girl wonders what it'd
be like to be a queen—including
princesses! When a princess secretly
tries on her mother's crown, the
crown should be too big.

POUTING PRINCESS
There are times when being a princess is just no fun—you're not allowed to get messy, nobody lets you do anything for yourself, you have to eat in the fancy dining room with all the boring dignitaries. You know how it is.

AROUND THE KINGDOM

L et's take a tour of a typical medieval village. What goes on behind the scenes?

Single curved line

Ordinary Village Folk

The villagers lived outside of the castle. They spent most of their time doing work like sweeping the streets, tying up horses, or delivering freshly baked bread.

WORKER
Notice that this man's shoulders aren't just stuck onto the torso. They form a single, curved line from shoulder to shoulder.

The Medieval Village

Medieval villages had short buildings, narrow streets, and merchants selling all kinds of goods.

YE OLDE BAKE SHOPPE

HALT!

Most castles, even small ones, had moats and drawbridges. If not, they didn't last long.

Castle Corridors

Castles were full of hallways, secret passageways, and shadowy places in which to hide and lurk!

The King Knights a Loyal Subject

Knighthood was a reward for loyalty and bravery. Knights lived within the castle. This was a great honor as it was much nicer there than in the noisy, crowded village.

MERLIN

Merlin is perhaps the most famous wizard of all time. You can recognize him right away by his long beard and sorcerer's outfit. Here, he weaves a magic spell.

MERLIN'S STUDY

Not many people knew how to read in medieval times. But Merlin did. To create his potions and spells, he would read from an old book of magic.

Secret Rendezvous

The *path of action* is the way you lead the eye through your picture. A clear path of action will help people understand what is happening. Here, we see the king looking at the lady, who is looking at the man, who is looking at the horse. The chain of events is clear: The king has come to court a young maiden, but doesn't know that she's just had a secret rendezvous with the hero.

DRAGONS

There is no clearer battle between good and evil than when a knight confronts a dark, evil dragon. And sometimes the knight must also battle his own horse, who would much rather turn tail and run!

Classic Dragon

Dragons can be drawn with or without wings and with various types of horns. They can be evil, sly, or even funny. And they can be any color you like. But they should always have sharp plates along their backs and long tails.

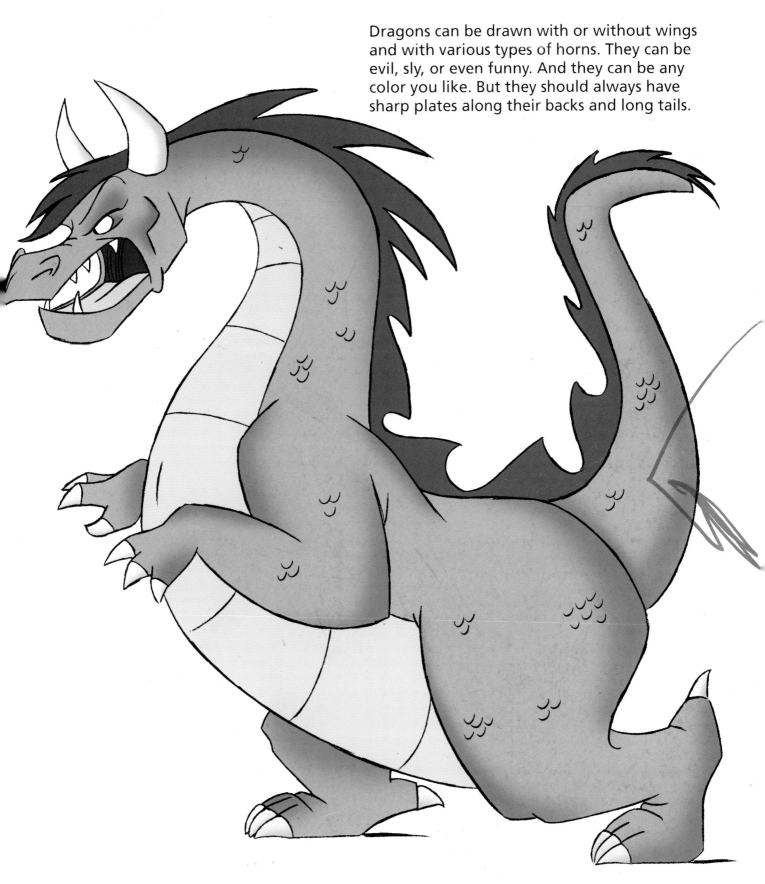

The Dragon's Head

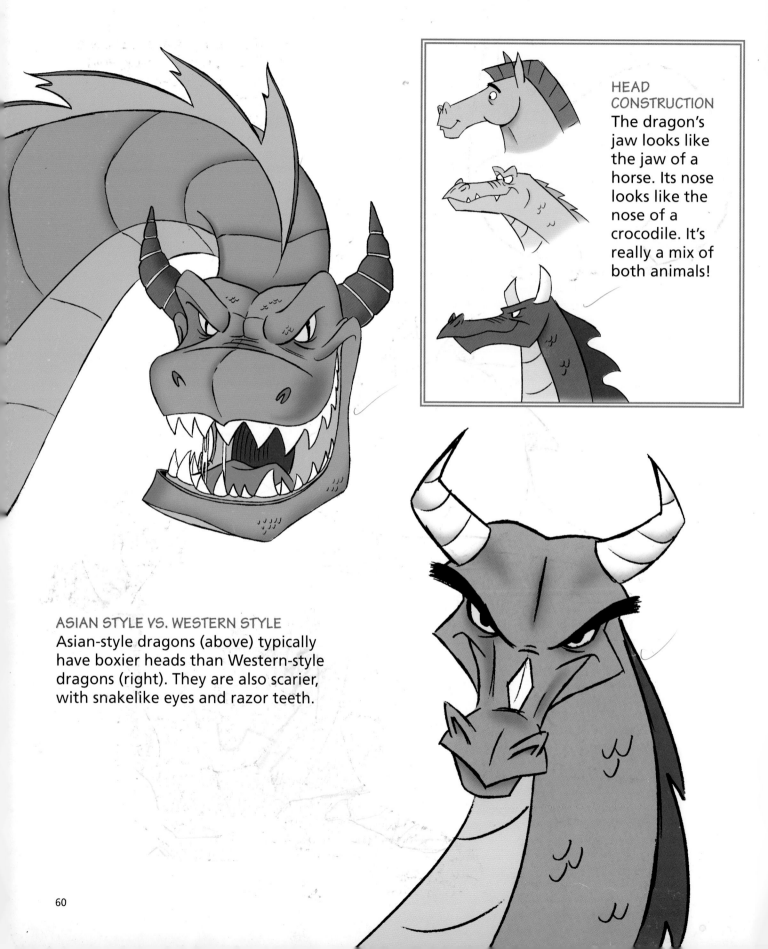

HEAD CONSTRUCTION
The dragon's jaw looks like the jaw of a horse. Its nose looks like the nose of a crocodile. It's really a mix of both animals!

ASIAN STYLE VS. WESTERN STYLE
Asian-style dragons (above) typically have boxier heads than Western-style dragons (right). They are also scarier, with snakelike eyes and razor teeth.

Silly Dragon

For this funny dragon, draw a small chin, narrow neck, and really fat body. Leave out the teeth or draw them sticking out, like rabbit's teeth.

Humorous Dragons

Go as far out as you want when inventing dragons! You can even dress them in modern-day clothes or put them in modern settings.

MOODY
Some dragons are always cranky.

YOUNG
Everybody loves a baby dragon.

OUT OF SHAPE
Even dragons have a sweet tooth!

ATHLETIC
This dragon's a winter sportsman.

GOOFY
A long tongue and close-set eyes give this dragon a goofy look.

Wings on a dragon look really cool. Not all wings need to be big enough for flying. Some, like the ones on this dragon, are just for decoration.

Few things are scarier than a flying dragon—except maybe a visit to the dentist. A flying dragon must have huge wings to support its body. When it flies, its legs are cradled below. Its head is lowered, looking down for the next victim. Yikes!

INDEX